ECOCRAFTS
Gorgeous Gifts

ECOCRAFTS
Gorgeous Gifts

KINGFISHER

KINGFISHER

Kingfisher Publications Plc
New Penderel House
283-288 High Holborn
London WC1V 7HZ
www.kingfisherpub.com

First published by Kingfisher Publications Plc 2007
2 4 6 8 10 9 7 5 3 1
1TR/0107/C&C/MAR(MAR)/128OJIEX-GREEN/C

Author: Rebecca Craig

For Toucan
Editor: Theresa Bebbington
Design: Leah Germann
Additional Makes by: Dawn Brend,
Melanie Williams, Kirsty Neale
Photography Art Direction: Jane Thomas
Editorial Assistant: Hannah Bowen
Photographer: Andy Crawford
Editorial Director: Ellen Dupont

For Kingfisher
Editorial Manager: Russell Mclean
Art Director: Mike Davis
Senior Production Controller: Lindsey Scott
DTP Coordinator: Catherine Hibbert

A CIP catalogue record for this book is available
from the British Library.

ISBN 978 07534 1453 8

Printed in China

**The paper used for the cover and text pages is
made from 100% recycled post consumer waste.**

Contents

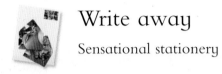

Eco-wise

When you give a gift that you have made yourself, you are giving a special present. It's a one-off. There won't be another one in the world just like it! And the person you give it to will love it because you took the time to make it for them.

As well as being really special, all the gifts in this book help the environment by using everyday things found in your home. A lot of them are things you would have thrown away. Inside you'll find ways to use an old jumper and some cardboard to make a shiny mouse mat, newspaper and cardboard to make a bright bangle, or even an old crisp packet to make a gift bag. Recycling helps the planet because it reuses things that would have ended up in the trash.

Around the world, tonnes of rubbish end up in landfills each year. In fact, in 1999 the

Fresh Kills landfill in New York City became the largest man-made structure in the world, overtaking the Great Wall of China. Because air and water cannot reach the rubbish buried deep in the landfill, the rubbish does not decompose, or break down. Even after 30 years you can still read newspapers buried in a landfill!

Sometimes rubbish goes to an incinerator, where it is burned. But this isn't a good solution either. The ashes still have to be disposed of – and they can be toxic. Burning rubbish also creates air pollution. The only really good way to reduce waste is to recycle. For example, by recycling plastic, 50 per cent less energy is used than if it was burned in an incinerator. And the plastic is used to make something else, such as a fleece jacket or even a park bench.

What you can do

Unwrap a present carefully so you can reuse the wrapping paper. Save the bows and ribbons to wrap another gift.

Cut up some card to make gift tags and then decorate them.

Use your old drawings, paintings and other artwork as wrapping paper. You can also reuse old newspaper or maps as wrapping paper.

Save cardboard boxes from your toys, shoes or even sweets. You can reuse them by putting gifts in them and then decorating or wrapping the boxes.

When buying a gift, buy one that is more durable. It can last longer than several cheaper versions, so fewer items will end up in a landfill.

Getting started

Before starting a project, make sure you have everything you need. If you don't know how to trace a picture or make papier-mâché, follow the steps here. Some craft supplies are not meant for children under 13 to use. If you're not sure if something is safe to use, ask an adult if it's okay. When using craft supplies that have a strong odour, work in a room that has plenty of fresh air. If an object is difficult to cut, ask an adult to help.

ruler

scissors

pen

pencil

paintbrush

tape

paint

PVA glue

TRACING A PICTURE

If you have a pencil, pen, tracing paper and tape, you can copy any picture you want. The pencil should have soft lead – this will make it easier to do the rubbing over the back. Use a pen with a hard point to make the lines really crisp.

STEP 1

Tape down a sheet of tracing paper over the picture you want to draw. Using a pen with a hard point, copy the picture onto the tracing paper.

STEP 2

Remove the tracing paper from the picture. Rub a soft-lead pencil on the back of the tracing paper where you can see the lines you have drawn.

STEP 3

Tape the paper onto the object where you want the picture. Draw over the lines in pen. Remove the tracing paper. The design will be on the object.

MAKING PAPIER-MÂCHÉ

By soaking newspaper in a paste made from flour and water, you can mould and build up many shapes. Use long strips of newspaper when you need to add strength.

The smaller pieces of newspaper are easier for moulding. Build up layers until you have the shape you want. Let the paper dry completely before decorating it.

STEP 1

Measure out one part of flour to about two parts of water. For example, use 125 grams of flour and 450 millilitres of water. Mix 4 tablespoons of salt with the flour to prevent the papier-mâché going mouldy.

STEP 2

Pour the water over the flour. Mix with a wooden spoon until you have a smooth paste without lumps – it should look like thick glue. If it is too thick, add a little more water. If it is too thin, add some more flour.

STEP 3

Rip up some newspaper into chunks or strips, following the steps for your project. Dip a chunk or strip of newspaper into the paste until it is really soaked. It is now ready to use.

Starry jars

You can transform an old jar into a beautiful tea light. If you want to paint the tea light with nail varnish, ask your parents first and paint in an airy room.

YOU WILL NEED:

small glass jar, scrubbing brush, cardboard, pen, scissors, nail varnish (or thin water-based acrylic paint or glass paint), paintbrush, garden wire (for hanging the tea light)

ECOFACT
Recycling just one glass bottle saves enough energy to run a computer for 25 minutes or a television for 90 minutes. Glass made from new materials creates more water pollution than glass made from recycled ingredients.

STEP 1

Clean out the jar carefully. First let it soak in soapy water to help remove the label, then scrub off the label. Let the jar dry completely.

STEP 2

Cut a long strip of cardboard that is the same height as your jar – but don't include the 'neck' of the jar. You can use a pen and ruler to mark where to cut the cardboard, then cut it with a pair of scissors.

10

STEP 3

To get the right length for the cardboard strip, wrap it snugly round the jar. Then draw a line with the pen where the end meets the cardboard. Remove the cardboard and cut along this line with your scissors.

STEP 4

Draw a design on the cardboard strip with a pen. Stars and a moon have been used here but draw anything you wish – why not try animals, flowers or rocket ships.

STEP 5

Roll up the cardboard with the design facing outwards. Place it inside the jar (you'll use it to copy your design onto the jar). Make sure the cardboard sits straight.

STEP 6

Paint your design onto the jar by following the design on the cardboard. Let the paint dry and remove the cardboard. Your tea light is ready for a candle!

Starry jars

STEP 7
For the hanger:
Ask a grown-up to cut a long piece of garden wire. Twist the ends together to form a loop. Centre the wire around the jar's 'neck', then twist tightly at both sides so that the wire grips the jar.

STEP 8
Twist the wire together, all the way down to the ends, until it is completely twisted – but leave a little loop in one end.

STEP 9
Feed the twisted end into the loop in the other end. Then twist it back around itself to fasten the two ends together.

Starry jar tea lights have a pretty glow when the candles are lit in the evening. Ask an adult to help you hang them in a safe place.

Hang several starry jar tea lights together for a spectacular night-time display.

13

Potty about plants

Make a funky plant pot for your mum, auntie or granny. This is a really fun and easy project and a great way to recycle yogurt pots or other plastic containers.

YOU WILL NEED:
yogurt pot (or other plastic container), PVA glue, paintbrush, string, scissors, paint, ribbon

ECOFACT
Many countries send plastic waste to China, but not (as some people believe) to be dumped in landfills. Because China makes lots of plastic goods, they need recyclable plastics to make things.

STEP 1
Turn the pot upside down and use a paintbrush to spread an even layer of glue all over the outside.

STEP 2
Start to wind the string round the pot, beginning at the base. Make sure the end of the string is tucked firmly under the first two or three wraps. Wind the string tightly, with no gaps.

Don't forget to water the plant after you plant it.

STEP 3

Continue winding the string round the pot until you reach the rim. Using scissors, trim off any extra string, and tuck the end neatly under the last few wraps of string to hide it. Let the glue dry completely.

STEP 4

Paint the flowerpot any colour you like. If you want a really neat finish, ask an adult to spray paint the pot. When the paint is dry, tie a ribbon around the pot, making a neat bow.

When planting the pot, don't fill it with soil all the way to the rim – leave some room for the water.

15

On your marks

Do you have a brother, sister or friend who always has his or her nose in a book? A pretty bookmark made from coffee stirrers would make a great gift.

YOU WILL NEED:

coffee stirrers (or disposable chopsticks or lolly sticks), colourful string (or ribbon or embroidery thread), scissors, bulldog clip

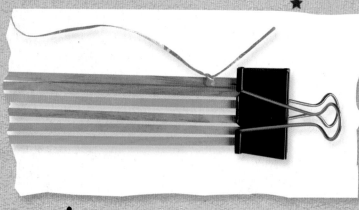

STEP 1

Ask an adult to put five or six coffee stirrers into a bulldog clip – this will hold them firmly as you work. Tie the end of the string to the first stirrer, near the edge of the clip.

STEP 2

Weave your string under and over each coffee stirrer until you reach the last stirrer.

16

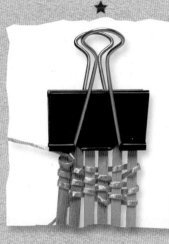

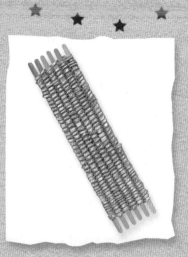

STEP 3

Wrap the string round the last stirrer, then continue weaving in the opposite direction. Make sure you weave under and over in an opposite pattern from the previous row of weaving.

STEP 4

Continue weaving the rows as in step 3, changing the weaving pattern for each row, until you reach the end of the stirrers.

STEP 5

Knot the end of the string around the last stirrer to fix it in place. You can also make a tassle by adding a few extra lengths of string to the knotted end.

Strings in different colours will make your bookmark stand out.

17

Brilliant bangle

This bangle is made entirely out of scrap paper, but don't worry – once it's dry, the bangle will be as solid as a rock and ready for you to decorate however you wish.

ECOFACT
Newspaper can be recycled up to seven times before its fibres become too short to make paper. Recycling paper creates 50 per cent less pollution than making new paper.

YOU WILL NEED:
....
cardboard, scissors, pencil, ruler, tape, newspaper, flour and water paste, paintbrush, PVA glue, glossy magazines, varnish (optional)

STEP 1

Cut a strip of cardboard as wide as you want your bangle and long enough to fit over your hand or the hand of the person who will wear it. Use a pencil and ruler to draw straight lines as a cutting guide.

STEP 2

Form a circle from the cardboard strip and tape the ends together. The circle should be a little large so there's room for the papier-mâché.

STEP 3

Mix up a flour and water paste (see page 9). Tear some newspaper into long strips, about the width of a finger. To make the bangle strong, tear some wider chunks as well.

18

STEP 4

Cover the strips with paste and wind them round the bangle. Make sure the newspaper is smooth, with no bumps, and well coated in paste.

STEP 5

To make your bangle chunky, scrunch up a sheet of newspaper into a thick strip and paste it round the outside of the bangle.

STEP 6

Cover the outer chunk with smaller strips of newspaper until it is smooth. Let the bangle dry overnight. Once dry, it will be hard and firm.

STEP 7

Dip strips cut out from a magazine in PVA glue and wrap them round the bangle. Once the glue is dry, your bangle is ready to wear.

For a really shiny finish, ask a grown-up to cover your bangle with a coat of varnish.

You can decorate your bangles by painting them, or by adding pictures from magazines, such as these flowers or butterfly shapes.

19

Sock puppy puppets

Why not recycle your old socks and turn them into a great gift for a younger brother or sister. With a little imagination your old socks can become anything you like. Will your puppet have teeth? Eyebrows? Whiskers? A moustache?

YOU WILL NEED:

old sock, pen, scissors, scraps of fabric and/or felt, elastic bands, three buttons, needle and thread, PVA glue, paint, paintbrush

STEP 1

Lie the sock out flat, mark a line on the sock halfway down the toes with a pen, then cut along the line with scissors. Repeat on the other side, so there are two slits.

STEP 2

Fit the sock over your hand. To make the mouth, push the end of the sock inside, until all the fabric up to the end of the slits nearest the heel is inside the sock. The slits will make the mouth less bulky.

STEP **3**

Draw an oval shape onto the fabric. Make sure it will be large enough to fit over the puppet's mouth. Cut out the oval shape.

STEP **4**

Spread some glue on one side of the oval-shaped fabric. Place the oval over the mouth, with the glued side facing the sock. Make sure the slits are not creeping out from behind the oval.

STEP **5**

To make the dog's ears, fold a piece of fabric or felt in half. Cut a long, thin oval in the fabric — these will make two identical ears.

Sock puppy puppets

STEP 6

Glue the ears on either side of the heel of the sock. Let the glue dry. (To make them really secure, ask an adult to sew them once the glue is dry.)

STEP 7

Cut out a shaggy shape from fabric or felt to make the dog's eye patch. Make it any shape you want. Glue the patch where you will be placing an eye (see step 10).

STEP 8

Cut out a piece of red fabric to make the tongue. Glue it inside the mouth. (Again, you can ask an adult to sew the tongue to make it secure once the glue is dry.)

STEP 9

For a brilliant finishing touch, cut a pair of elastic bands so they no longer form loops, then thread them through a large button to make a nose with whiskers.

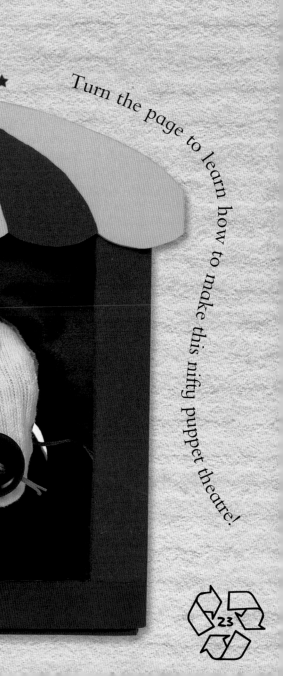

STEP 10

Ask an adult to sew on a pair of buttons as eyes and the larger button as a nose. Dab a blob of black paint on the lighter coloured buttons to make the eyes really stand out.

Turn the page to learn how to make this nifty puppet theatre!

Although we've made a puppy, you can follow these steps to create all sorts of exciting puppet animals, such as a fierce dragon or a cute little kitten.

23

Curtain up

You can transform a large cardboard box into a fantastic puppet theatre – a perfect place to show off a pair of funky sock puppy puppets (turn to page 20 to make this project).

YOU WILL NEED:
....
cardboard box, PVA glue, ruler, pencil, scissors, paint, paintbrush, thick card, black fabric, white chalk, velvet fabric, gold cord, small knitting needle

STEP 1
If your box has any open ends, glue them shut. Then, use a ruler and pencil to draw a narrow border around one large side. Cut out the area inside your pencil lines.

STEP 2
Draw two circles onto the back of the box, near the bottom. Cut them out, then check that the holes left behind are big enough to comfortably fit your hand (and puppet) through.

24

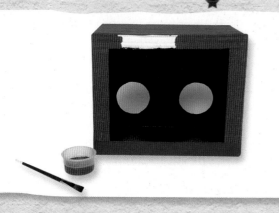

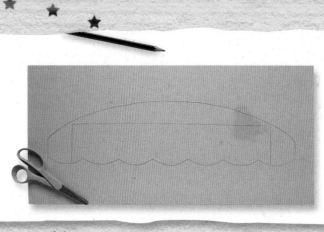

STEP 3

Paint the inside of your box black. Once dry, add another coat and let it dry. Then paint a dark colour along the top, back and sides of the box and the bottom edge of the 'frame'. Let it dry, then add a bright paint to the top and side edges of the frame.

STEP 4

Trace the shape of the top of your box onto thick card. Using this as a guide, draw a curvy pediment around it – it will sit above your theatre stage. Cut the pediment out.

STEP 5

In pencil, draw stripes that curve outwards from the top to the bottom. The direction of the curve will change in the middle of the pediment.

STEP 6

Using a paintbrush, paint every other stripe a bright colour such as yellow. Then paint the remaining stripes in a contrasting bright colour.

Curtain up

STEP 7

Brush plenty of glue along the top edge of the frame on your box. Carefully press the pediment on top of it, making sure it's centred. Lie the box on its back while the glue dries so the pediment does not fall off.

STEP 8

Draw round the back of your box onto a piece of black fabric. A white chalk line will be easy to see. Cut the fabric out and brush PVA glue along all four edges. Allow to dry. This stops the fabric from fraying.

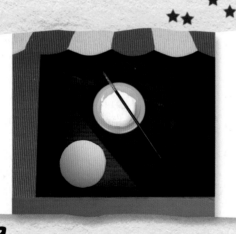

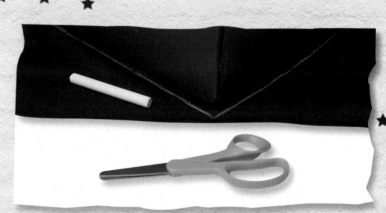

STEP 9

Spread glue along one long edge of the fabric on the side that you will not see. Press it along the top of the back wall, inside the box. Lie the box flat until the glue is dry.

STEP 10

Draw round the back of the box onto the back of some velvet. Make the bottom edge 5 centimetres longer, then cut it out. Fold the fabric in half and cut along the fold. Seal the edges with PVA glue and allow to dry.

STEP 11

Add glue to the narrow edge of one piece, on the velvety side of the fabric. Press it into place behind the pediment, inside your box. Add the second curtain in the same way. Let the glue dry.

STEP 12

With a small knitting needle, make two small holes in one side of your box, near the front and about halfway up. They should be about 1.5 centimetres apart. Cut 25 centimetres of gold cord and poke the ends through the holes. Repeat on the other side of the box.

STEP 13

Pull each curtain to one side and use the cord to tie them in place.

If you can't find red velvet, purple or green will make dramatic curtains too.

The black cloth at the back of your stage will cover the holes when you are not using them. When you put your puppet through the hole, the material will gather up around your arm.

27

Magic magnet

You can turn the lid from an old jar into a magnet for the fridge. This is a great gift for mum or dad – and it's a neat way to recycle the leftover lid from the starry jar tea light (see pages 10–13).

YOU WILL NEED:
•••
polystyrene packaging, jar lid, felt-tip pen, scissors, PVA glue, paintbrush, photographs or magazines, magnet strips

ECOFACT

The lids of glass jars need to be removed before recycling the glass. In most areas, these lids are not recyclable. Thinking up new ways of using the lids, such as these magnets, will mean that fewer lids end up in landfills.

STEP 1

Place the lid of a jar on top of the polystyrene packaging and draw round it with a pen.

STEP 2

Cut out the circle just slightly smaller than the one you have drawn – this way it will fit inside the lid.

STEP 3

To cut out a picture the same size as your polystyrene circle, put the circle over it, draw round the circle and cut out the picture.

STEP 4

Spread glue onto the polystyrene circle and glue the picture to it.

STEP 5

Put glue on the inside of the jar lid. Then press the picture onto it, making sure it is centred.

STEP 6

Glue a magnetic strip to the back of the lid so it will stick to the fridge. Your magnet is now ready to be used.

Make a set of matching magnets by using similar pictures cut out of magazines, such as a set of flowers, sports cars or your favourite pop stars.

Parents always like photos of their kids, but make sure it's okay to use them.

29

Bang the drum

A strong, round, empty container will make a great drum for a budding musician in the family. Make sure your container is empty and clean before you start the project!

YOU WILL NEED:

large round container, paint, paintbrushes, pencil, small ruler, greaseproof paper, small bowl or saucer, PVA glue, tissue paper, coloured elastic (or hair) bands

STEP 1
Paint your container white all over and allow it to dry. You don't have to worry about making this layer of paint too neat — it's just to help with the next stage.

STEP 2

Using a small ruler and a pencil, draw vertical stripes on the white background. You can make them all different widths, or if you prefer, the same size.

STEP 3

Paint every other stripe, alternating between colours of your choice. Bright colours will stand out more.

STEP 4

When the painted stripes are completely dry, fill in the ones between them with two more paint colours. Allow these to dry, too.

STEP 5

For the skin of the drum, place a bowl that is a few centimetres wider than your drum on some greaseproof paper and draw round it. Cut out the circle.

Bang the drum

STEP 6

Spread glue all over one side of the circle. Use lots of glue and spread it out smoothly. This will make the drum skin tight.

STEP 7

While the glue is wet, stretch the greaseproof paper over the top of the drum as tightly as you can, with the extra paper folded down the sides of the drum.

STEP 8

Cut a circle from some colourful tissue paper, just as you did from the greaseproof paper. Brush glue all over one side and smooth it over the paper on top of your drum.

STEP 9

To hold the greaseproof paper and tissue in place as they dry, and to add some extra decoration, carefully stretch one or two coloured elastic bands around the sides of the drum. Or try using stretched-out hair bands.

You can paint your drums any pattern you like. Or cut out shapes, such as stars, circles or flowers, from colourful wrapping paper and glue them on the drum.

Make a set of drums by using containers of different sizes.

Write away

Is there someone who loves writing letters in your family? Surprise them with their own personalized stationery set made from discarded envelopes and magazines. It's a neat way to recycle!

YOU WILL NEED:
··
envelope from a Christmas or birthday card, tracing paper, tape, ruler, pen, pencil, cardboard, scissors, A4 envelopes, magazine pictures, glue stick

STEP 1
Carefully take apart an old envelope to use it to make a template. Trace round the envelope and its folds onto tracing paper. Transfer it to cardboard (see page 8).

STEP 2
Cut out the template, taking extra care around any little indentations at the corners. Put the template over a large piece of magazine paper, draw round it and cut along the lines.

34

STEP 3

Fold in the bottom flap. Now fold in the two side flaps and stick them to the bottom flap using a glue stick.

STEP 4

Now make the writing paper. On the back of a used A4 envelope, draw a rectangle with a pencil and ruler. It should be large enough for writing a letter.

STEP 5

Use a pair of scissors to cut the paper along the rectangle. Try to keep the lines as straight as you can.

STEP 6

To decorate the writing paper, cut out pictures from a magazine. Cut them into small squares or other shapes. Glue them to the paper – make sure you leave space for writing!

35

High flier

You can use a takeaway container to make a flying aeroplane that will zoom around your room! Make sure you clean the container and let it dry first.

YOU WILL NEED:
tracing paper, pencil, ruler, cardboard, scissors, polystyrene container, felt-tip pen, paint, paintbrush, paperclip

ECOFACT
Polystyrene, used to make takeaway food containers, cannot be recycled. This plastic often drifts into drains and sewers. Then it flows into the sea and breaks up into tiny pieces. It can be eaten by marine life, which may die from it.

STEP 1
Trace the templates for the plane (see page 46), using a pencil and tracing paper to transfer them to cardboard (see page 8).

STEP 2
Cut out the cardboard templates with a pair of scissors, cutting carefully to keep the lines straight.

STEP 3
Place the templates on top of your polystyrene container. Draw round them with a felt-tip pen.

STEP 4
Carefully cut out the three plane shapes from the polystyrene using a pair of sharp scissors.

STEP **5**

Ask an adult to use a craft knife to cut two slits in the body of the plane, just wide enough to fit the wings.

STEP **6**

Paint any pattern you like on the pieces of the plane. Let the paint dry on one side before painting the other side.

STEP **7**

To assemble the plane, push the small wings into the slit at the back of the body and the big wings into the slit at the front.

STEP **8**

Push a paperclip onto the nose of the plane. This will add weight to the front of the plane, which will help it to fly.

Then paint a cockpit for the pilot – choose any colours you want.

Your plane is now ready for a test flight!

Bright lights

You can make an amazing window decoration by cutting silhouette shapes out of two layers of black paper and using colourful sweet wrappers to create the 'stained glass'.

YOU WILL NEED:
··
tracing paper, pen, white chalk or grease pencil, black card or paper, scissors, see-through sweet wrappers, glue stick or tape, PVA glue, paintbrush

STEP 1
Trace the leaf design (see page 47) onto tracing paper (see page 8).

STEP 2
Rub a white pencil over the back of the tracing and transfer the stencil onto the black paper.

STEP 3
To cut out a 'window pane', fold the paper gently over, making sure it doesn't crease. Cut into the fold, in an area that will be a pane. Unfold the paper and continue the cut to a line, then cut along the line.

STEP 4

Repeat step 3 until you have cut out all of the window panes.

STEP 5

Turn the black paper over. Cut a sweet wrapper so it fits snugly over a pane, and tape or glue it down. Repeat this step for each pane.

STEP 6

If you want a glossy finish, spread glue over your window. Let it dry.

Hang your stencil in a window that gets lots of light.

We have used a leaf pattern, but you can use other stencils or make your own. Why not try a rabbit, a rocket ship, or stars and a crescent moon?

39

Mighty mouse

Why not make a mouse mat for a computer-mad friend or relative? Our mouse mat features a cute mouse, but you can draw your own design instead.

YOU WILL NEED:
tracing paper, pencil, strong card (the card from a board-backed envelope is perfect), scissors, paint, paintbrushes, waterproof black felt-tip pen, PVA glue, old woollen jumper or blanket, thin paper, pins

STEP 1
Trace the mouse template on page 43, including the eyes, ears, nose, mouth and whiskers. Transfer the tracing to a piece of thick card (see page 8).

STEP 2
Neatly cut round the outside edges of the card. Make sure you take care at the corners around the ears.

STEP 3

Paint the mouse's face and the edges of its ears a light colour. Don't worry about going over the mouth and whiskers – when the paint dries, you will still be able to see the faint marks made by pressing your pencil down.

STEP 4

When the paint is dry, use a small brush to paint the centre of the ears a bright colour, the nose a pale colour and the eyes white. Allow it to dry.

STEP 5

With a black felt-tip pen, carefully outline the eyes and add pupils. Outline the nose and the centre of the ears, then draw on the mouth and whiskers.

STEP 6

To protect your mat and give it a glossy finish, brush on two or three coats of PVA glue. Spread the glue smoothly, but not too thinly. Allow each coat to dry before adding the next.

Mighty mouse

STEP 7

Ask an adult to wash your woolly item on the hottest cycle in a washing machine. The wool will turn to felt and be smaller when it comes out. It will also feel thicker and won't fray when you cut it. Let the felted wool dry.

STEP 8

Trace the mouse again – this time onto a piece of thin scrap paper – and cut it out.

STEP 9

Pin the paper shape to your felted wool. Cut round the mouse shape.

STEP 10

Cover the back of your cardboard mouse with PVA glue. Carefully place the felt mouse shape on top and smooth it down. Rest books on top of the mat until the glue dries.

The smooth surface makes the mat ideal for a computer mouse.

Mouse mat template

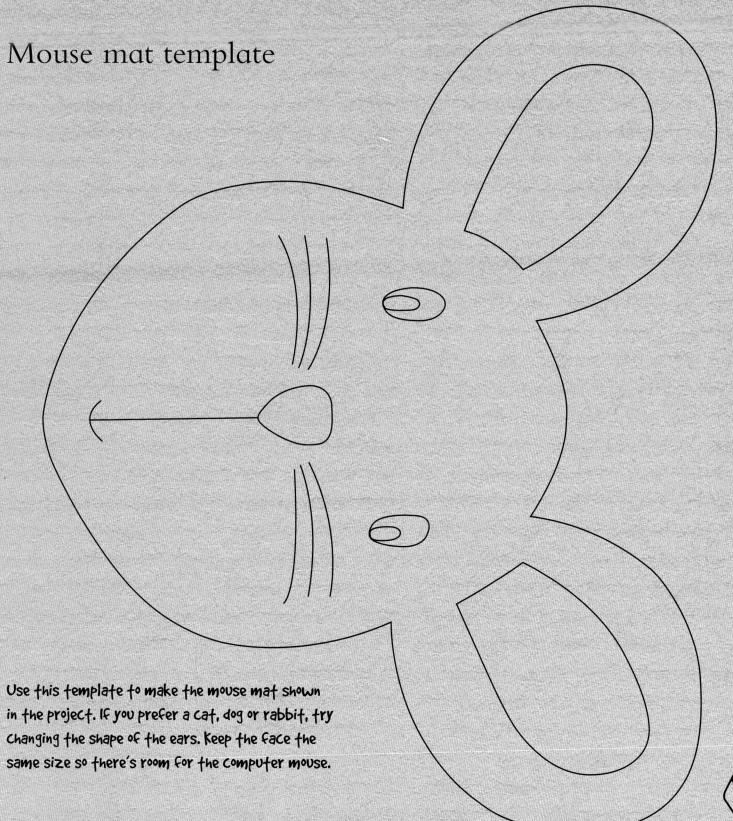

Use this template to make the mouse mat shown in the project. If you prefer a cat, dog or rabbit, try changing the shape of the ears. Keep the face the same size so there's room for the computer mouse.

43

# It's a wrap

Now that you've made some great presents, how will you wrap them up? Here's a cool way to reuse a crisp packet for a sturdy gift. (It's not ideal for delicate gifts such as silk scarves!)

YOU WILL NEED:
••••••••••••••••••••••••••••••••••••••
crisp packet (with shiny foil inside), paper towel, tape, ribbon or string, scissors

STEP 1

Give a large crisp packet a good wash with washing-up liquid. Let the packet dry. Turn it inside out by pushing the bottom of the packet through the top half.

STEP 2

Use a paper towel to give your packet a rub to make sure all traces of food have been removed. If the paper towel becomes dirty or greasy, clean your packet again. Allow the packet to dry.

STEP 3

Turn 7.5 to 10 centimetres of the top edge over, inside the packet. Tape it down to create a finished edge.

STEP 4

Place your gift inside the packet. Cut a piece of ribbon or coloured string. Tie it round the packet and make a large, neat bow.

Fluff out the packet above the ribbon to give it a finishing touch.

45

Leaf template

(for pages 38–39)

47

Index